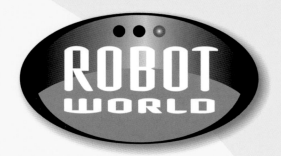

Robots
on the Move

by Steve Parker

amicus

Published by Amicus
P.O. Box 1329
Mankato, MN 56002

Printed in the United States of America, at
Corporate Graphics in North Mankato, Minnesota.

Library of Congress Cataloging-in-Publication Data
Parker, Steve, 1952-
   Robots on the move / by Steve Parker.
      p. cm. – (Robot world)
   Includes index.
   Summary: "Discusses the latest advancements in
robotics and how they are made to move in
different ways"–Provided by publisher.
   ISBN 978-1-06735-076-3 (library binding)
   1. Mobile robots–Juvenile literature. I. Title.
   TJ211.415.P36 2011
   629.8'932–dc22

                                    2010001123

Created by Appleseed Editions Ltd.
Designed by Guy Callaby
Edited by Mary-Jane Wilkins
Picture research by Su Alexander

Picture acknowledgements
Title page AFP/Getty Images; contents page John Hicks/Corbis;
4 Maximilian Stock Ltd/Science Photo Library; 5 Mode Images
Ltd/Alamy; 6 & 7 Getty Images; 8 Vaughn Youtz/Zuma/Corbis;
9t AFP/Getty Images, b Jochen Luebke/epa/Corbis;
10 Maximilian Stock Ltd/Science Photo Library; 11l Volker
Moehrke/Corbis, r Philippe Plailly/Eurelios/Science Photo
Library; 12 National Geographic/Getty Images; 13t Vaughn
Youtz/Zuma/Corbis, b Izmostock/Alamy; 14t Julian Calder/
Corbis, b Car Culture/Corbis; 15 Culture-Images GmbH/
Alamy; 16 DARPA; 17 AFP/Getty Images; 18 Getty Images;
19t Getty Images, b John Hicks/Corbis; 20 Gianni Muratore/
Alamy; 21t David Hodges/Alamy, b Photos 12/Alamy;
22 © Colin Sauze 2007; 23 Karen Kasmauski/Corbis;
24 Louie Psihoyos/Corbis; 25 Peter Ginter/Science Faction/
Corbis; 26 Chris Carroll/Corbis; 27t Jerry Lampen/Reuters/
Corbis, b Peter Ginter/Science Faction/Corbis; 28 GSFC/
NASA; 29t GSFC/NASA, b ESA-J Huart
Front cover Peter Menzel/Science Photo Library

DAD0040
32010

9 8 7 6 5 4 3 2 1

Contents

Robots Go!

Some robots stay in one place and can't move around. But others are rarely still. These robots go places and do things, often by themselves, without needing our help. That's partly what makes them robots.

Why Travel?

Most robots have gears, motors, levers, and similar moving parts inside. These whirr and spin and **pivot**. But not all robots can move themselves from place to place on wheels or legs. Robots that travel are called mobile, roving, active, or **locomotory robots**.

Mobile robots move around for a reason. Designers and engineers build them to carry out particular jobs or tasks, which need them to go from one place to another. Giving a robot wheels or legs when it does not really need them would be a waste of effort, time, energy, and money.

Robot trucks and carriers called automated guided vehicles (AGVs) carry items around factories, stores, and warehouses. They follow guide wires buried under the floor.

Energy Needs

A roving robot is much more complicated than one which is stationary or fixed in one place. Not only does a mobile robot need wheels, legs, or other mechanical parts to move around, it also needs the energy to move. This may come from an onboard energy source, such as a battery. The robot also needs to be able to find its way, or navigate, and to avoid bumps and crashes that might damage it or objects around it—including people. Safety is important when robots travel around.

Robot Helpers

Some robots travel long distances but don't have wheels, legs, or similar parts. These are onboard robots for ships, trains, planes, trucks, wagons, and other vehicles. Sometimes they operate alone and are in command, with no people. In other cases, the robots are partly automatic and act as helpers for human pilots, drivers, and riders.

If the human pilot switched off the radio controller, this model plane would soon crash. It cannot fly safely on its own, unlike a true robot aircraft.

ROBOT OR NOT?

Total Control

Many people play with radio-controlled (RC) model cars, trucks, planes, and ships. Are these true robots? Not usually. Most move around according to the instructions of the operator, who controls their speed and direction, second by second. Real robots control themselves and work automatically to some extent.

How Robots Move

Humans can walk, jump, hop, and run. Some robots can walk, and a very few can even run. But most robots move around in other ways. Many roll along on wheels. There are robots that trundle on rollers and rumble on crawler tracks. And there are robots with propellers that fly through the sky, swish across water, or even float on air like a hovercraft.

Champion Rollers

Pal and Chum are real robo-sprinters. They are 4.3 feet (1.3 m) tall and speak about 100 words. Balancing expertly on two wheels, they can race along at more than 3.7 miles per hour (6 km/h)— about as fast as you could jog.

▼ *Soryu the snake is a rescue robot with sets of crawler tracks, which allow it to travel in awkward places. It searches for people at disaster sites, such as in the rubble of a collapsed building, using its video camera eye.*

Wheeling Along

One of the best ways for robots to move around is to roll on wheels. But wheels work best on smooth surfaces such as floors, paths, and roads. They have trouble with lumpy, bumpy, and softer surfaces, such as soil, leaves, sand, and stones. Most wheeled robots can't go up or down a steep ramp or stairs. They have trouble even stepping over a curb.

Moving at a Crawl

Caterpillar tracks or crawler tracks can be an alternative to wheels for traveling over rough ground. But movement on these is slow and they need lots of power. So cat-track robots need huge batteries or a long wire connecting them to an electrical supply. Another option is to travel along rails, like a train. However, that limits where the robot can go.

Through Air and Water

For the robots that we send up into the sky, or over and under the sea, propellers are the best choice. On robo-planes, the props are often called air screws, and on robot ships, they are called water screws. This is because their twisted blades pull them along through air or water with a screw-like movement.

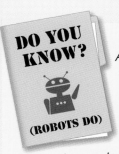

Travelers' Tales

Adventurous people travel to many remote places, such as mountain peaks and deep caves. Some mobile robots go on even stranger journeys. They burrow through soil, squeeze through long, narrow pipelines, and voyage through pitch-black, freezing underground rivers or oceans.

*The four-propeller AirRobot measures 39.4 inches (1 m) across and finds its way using global positioning system (**GPS**) satellite navigation. It can hover, take pictures with its three cameras, and send them back to base via radio signals. This makes it useful for checking accident scenes.*

Robo-rolling

Making a mobile robot with wheels turned by an electric motor sounds simple. But there are hundreds of sizes and types of wheels. There are also many different types of tires, as well as different electric motors, axles and bearings, gears, chains, steering methods—so it's not so simple.

Size Matters

Big wheels move a robot faster than small wheels, if the wheels turn at the same speed. Large wheels are heavier and harder for the motor to spin, so the motor needs to be more powerful so that it has more turning force, called **torque**. Big wheels work best on smooth surfaces. Smaller wheels work better on bumpy ground, but a small-wheeled robot can be so close to the ground that it gets stuck on bumps.

Outdoor robots need big tires with deep tread to cover rough ground. This is Terramax, an entrant in the DARPA Challenge (see page 16).

▼ *Halluc II rolls along on eight steerable wheels, each with an electric motor. Alternatively, it can lock all the wheels and walk along like a spider.*

Robots in Action■

HEALTH CHECK

Like other machines with moving parts, robots need regular checkups and servicing. Their wheel bearings get dirty and worn, especially if they travel over dirt and bumpy ground. Like levers, motors, and other parts, they need oil or grease so they run smoothly. Some robots are programmed to tell humans when service is due.■

Hard Rims

A wheel with a hard plastic or metal edge, called the rim, is strong and long-lasting. The problem with hard edges is that they can slip and skid easily on many surfaces. They also give a hard, jolting ride, which might shake and damage the robot's delicate parts inside.

Softer Edges

Rubber, soft plastic, or spongy foam tires are best for gripping. Robots that work outside need tires with a pattern of grooves called tread, like car or bicycle tires. The tread grips damp, slippery surfaces well. The problem with softer tires is that they wear out faster. If they are **pneumatic** (filled with air), like bicycle tires, sharp objects might puncture them. Few robots can mend their own punctures or change their own wheels!

ROBOT SUPERSTAR

Blue Max

One of the biggest and most fun fighting robots is Blue Max. It weighs as much as two people and has a big, deep-tread tire on each corner, for the best possible grip. Its main weapon is a sloping wedge at the front, which it pushes under rival robots to flip them over.

Motoring Along

More than 99 of every 100 mobile robots are powered by electric motors. The size of the motor depends on the robot's weight and the load it might have to carry. Big, heavy robots might have two motors, or even one for each wheel.

Gearing Up for Big Loads

Motors have a part that spins called the drive shaft, which can turn around hundreds of times per second. A wheel fixed to the shaft would spin so fast that the robot would zoom out of control and crash! So every motor has sets of **gears** called **reduction gears**. A small-toothed gear **cog** (gearwheel) on the motor's driveshaft spins fast, which turns a larger gearwheel attached to the wheel more slowly. This reduced speed gives more torque, so the robot can travel up hills or carry heavier loads.

▶▶ *The engines of big trucks and trains have massive gears to adjust the spinning speed and turning power (torque). Robots have smaller versions for the same purpose.*

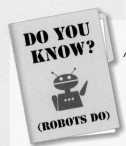

DO YOU KNOW?

(ROBOTS DO)

Talking Torque

A mobile robot relies on its electric motor. This makes its strongest turning force or torque when it is spinning fast.

The problem is that the robot needs the most turning force to start it moving when it is still. Certain robots feed more electricity into their motors when they start up, then reduce the amount as the robot speeds up. This gives a smoother ride and saves lots of battery power.

ROBO-FUTURE

Step into the Future

Scientists and engineers are always developing motors that last longer and use less energy. Small motors that turn around slowly and precisely, called stepper motors, are used for computer disc drives. Bigger, stronger versions would be a good choice for the newest robot designs.

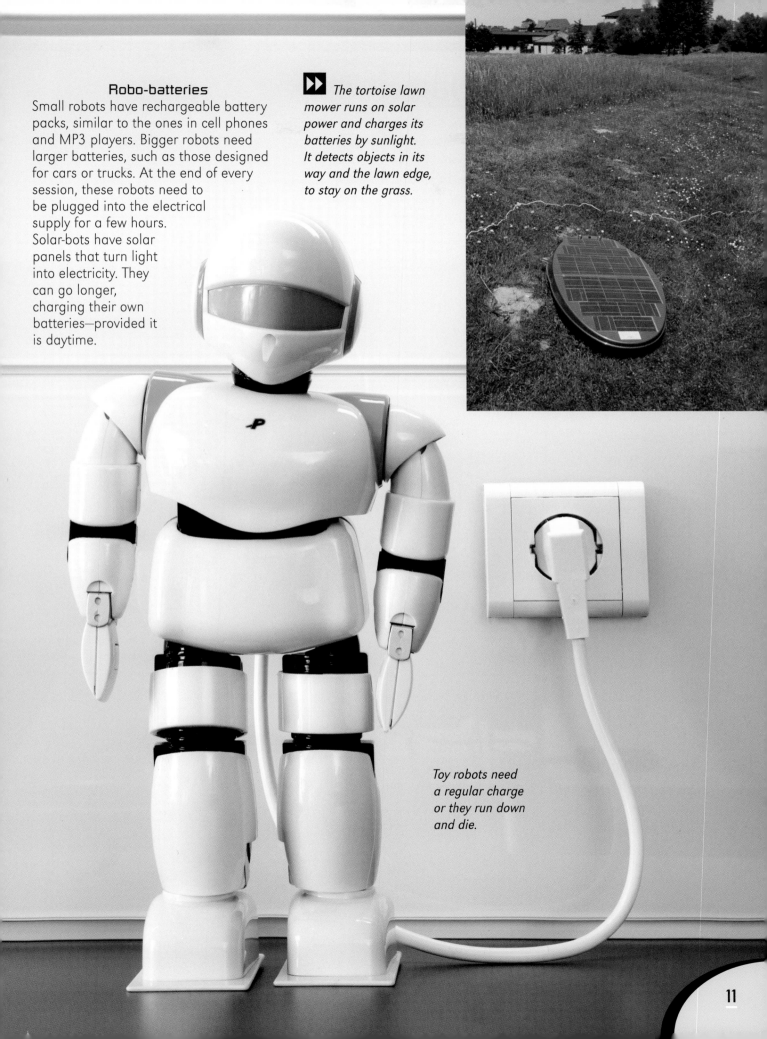

Robo-batteries

Small robots have rechargeable battery packs, similar to the ones in cell phones and MP3 players. Bigger robots need larger batteries, such as those designed for cars or trucks. At the end of every session, these robots need to be plugged into the electrical supply for a few hours. Solar-bots have solar panels that turn light into electricity. They can go longer, charging their own batteries—provided it is daytime.

▶▶ *The tortoise lawn mower runs on solar power and charges its batteries by sunlight. It detects objects in its way and the lawn edge, to stay on the grass.*

Toy robots need a regular charge or they run down and die.

Finding the Way

As we walk around, we automatically see objects in our way and avoid them. For a mobile robot, this is a great challenge. It needs to know where it is, where it's going, and find the way. This is known as **navigation**. It has to steer carefully and safely, and avoid danger, blows, and crashes.

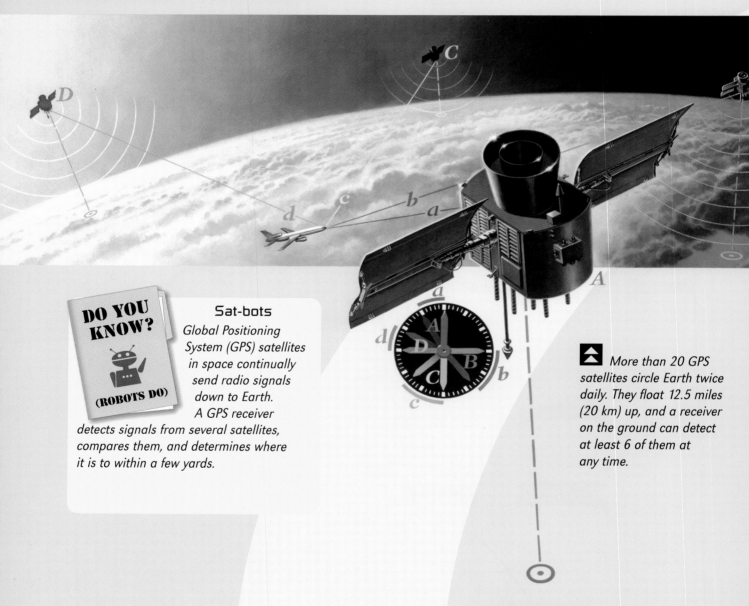

Sat-bots

Global Positioning System (GPS) satellites in space continually send radio signals down to Earth. A GPS receiver detects signals from several satellites, compares them, and determines where it is to within a few yards.

More than 20 GPS satellites circle Earth twice daily. They float 12.5 miles (20 km) up, and a receiver on the ground can detect at least 6 of them at any time.

What's Around?

Robots have many **sensors**. Humans have sensors too—our eyes and ears. Some robots have camera eyes which detect light around them and send the information to an onboard computer. This determines which objects it needs to avoid from their shapes and colors. If an object gradually grows larger in the camera's view, the robot determines that it is moving toward it.

Invisible Beams

Some robots have simpler ways of detecting nearby objects. They send out short bursts or **pulses** of beams, especially **laser beams** or invisible **infrared light** (the same as the beams used in TV remote controls). Laser or infrared sensors pick up any beams that bounce back, or reflect, from objects nearby. The direction and timing of the reflections show the size, shape, and distance of the object.

Where Am I Going?

Robots that move around the same area all the time usually have a map in their computer memory. Once they detect three or four familiar objects nearby, such as walls, machines, desks, or trees, they can determine where they are. Their computer program can then instruct them on how to steer to the destination. Bigger outdoor mobile robots usually have satellite navigation.

Robots in Action ■

KEEPING UP-TO-DATE

For robots that move around factories and warehouses, the map of the surroundings in their computer memory must be kept up-to-date. If human workers move cupboards, desks, crates, and other objects, then the robots need re-programming so they can figure out new routes to avoid the obstacles. ■

▲ *Outdoor robots such as Navigator rely on satellite navigation. If the GPS receiver fails, the robot stops.*

▼ *Many modern cars have a GPS or satellite navigation (satnav) receiver.*

Robots on the Road

Imagine it's rush hour in a big city. Traffic jams build up, drivers get annoyed, cyclists weave in and out, and people run between vehicles. Traveling by robo-car sounds like a good idea to take the strain out of driving. But could a robot handle so much going on?

▲ Busy roads mean human drivers must be alert to all kinds of sights and sounds. Robot drivers are not yet advanced or safe enough for these conditions.

▶▶ The Pivo 2 car of the future has a camera eye and microphone ear to check its human driver's face and voice. When the driver shows signs of stress, such as frowning or shouting, the little robot head suggests a break to calm down.

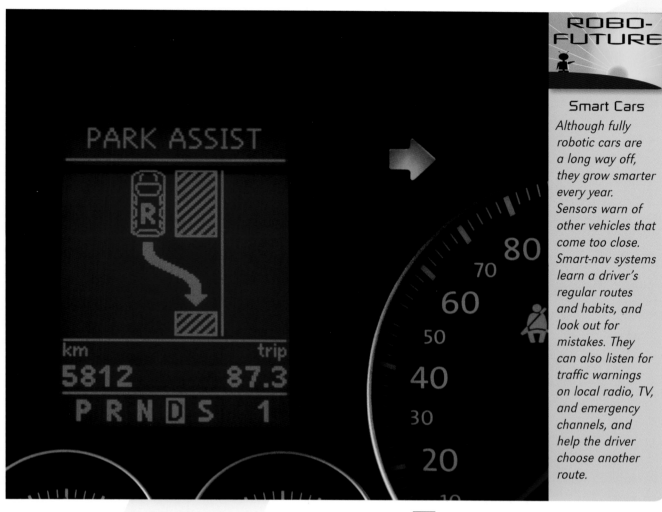

Smart Cars

Although fully robotic cars are a long way off, they grow smarter every year. Sensors warn of other vehicles that come too close. Smart-nav systems learn a driver's regular routes and habits, and look out for mistakes. They can also listen for traffic warnings on local radio, TV, and emergency channels, and help the driver choose another route.

An assisted parking device uses ultrasound sensors to detect the road edge and other vehicles, then shows the driver the best parking method.

Way to Go

A completely robotic car that drives itself on public roads, obeys traffic signs and signals, and avoids other vehicles and hazards, is probably many years away. There are simply too many actions to carry out and problems that might happen, such as a child running into the road. On the road, safety is the biggest concern, and today's robots are not sophisticated or reliable enough to travel on these roads. However, robot-style gadgets can help drivers in many ways. Some modern cars have breakdown warning systems, obstacle sensor beepers, and automatic parking controls. Intelligent satellite navigation can be programmed into the steering wheel so the driver feels which way to go, while staying in control.

Auto-trucks

Away from public roads, in places with less traffic such as quarries, mines, and industrial sites, robo-vehicles are becoming more common. Some of the biggest are huge mining trucks that weigh more than 551 tons (500 t)—12 times heavier than the biggest trucks on ordinary roads. They find their way by satnav and come to a quick stop if anything goes wrong.

DO YOU KNOW?

(ROBOTS DO)

Robot Road Cones

Lines of road cones and barriers mean roadwork or an accident ahead. Engineers are testing mobile versions with batteries and wheels, which can detect their position using radio signals. They are programmed to move around and make an exact pattern, for example, to close off a lane for safety as soon as a car breaks down.

Ultimate Challenge

One of the world's toughest robot contests held every few years is called the Grand Challenge. The contest is for robot cars without drivers and the prizes are worth millions of dollars.

Ghost Town

The Defense Advanced Research Projects Agency (DARPA) tests all kinds of weird and wacky ideas that might come in useful one day. Its Grand Challenge is held in a remote part of the Mojave Desert in California.

In 2007, DARPA held an urban challenge which had a route through a "city"—an air force base which had been closed down. The driverless robots faced challenges such as traveling over rough ground, steering between buildings, parking, avoiding other cars and people (in the form of cardboard cutouts), and moving through traffic.

In the 2007 Challenge, Lone Wolf (above) reverses to turn around while Talos (right) drives carefully along a pretend city street. Lone Wolf is a modified Lotus Elise with eight laser sensors. Talos is a Landrover LR3 with 13 laser sensors, 15 radar sensors, and 5 video cameras.

Failed Challenger

The DARPA Challenge car Alice became a star, because it failed in a big way. The car was a modified Ford E350 van built by the California Institute of Technology (CalTech). The car's satnav went haywire and Alice roared over a concrete barrier toward nearby spectators. But the human safety backup crew flicked the "kill" switch before Alice did any real damage.

Challenge Entrants

The robot that wins the Grand Challenge scores highest on speed, carrying out all tasks, and staying out of trouble. The vehicles control themselves for up to 10 hours with no human help. They have all kinds of sensors, including laser and infrared beams, cameras, the radio signals of radar, and satnav. Powerful electric motors work the steering wheel, accelerator, and brakes. The "brain" of the vehicle is a powerful computer that determines where to go and how fast, and which part of the challenge to try next. There are many built-in safety features to make sure the vehicles don't race off on their own across the desert.

Serious Business

Robot designers and engineers spend years and lots of money developing and building their robot cars, because the challenge has a serious side. It helps develop robot military vehicles which could carry supplies in war zones or even fight an enemy through city streets. This might save the lives of many soldiers.

▼ *The robot Chevrolet Tahoe named Boss won the 2007 Challenge, completing the course in 4 hours and 10 minutes. Its human team from Carnegie Mellon University and General Motors won the first prize of $2 million.*

Robots on Rails

Robot trains and other vehicles that run on rails can only go where the rails take them. Even so, they must start and stop correctly, control their speed, obey signals, and make sure they take the correct track where sets of rails meet at points.

Robot trains carry passengers back and forth at many main airports, seaports, theme parks, and other large sites. These trains are at Beijing Airport, China. Passengers can press an emergency button if there's a problem.

No Drivers

Several cities around the world have driverless railway train systems, including Beijing in China, Yongin in South Korea, Kuala Lumpur in Malaysia, Vancouver and Toronto in Canada, and Las Vegas, Detroit, and New York. They are called rapid mass transit, which means that the robot trains carry lots of people quickly around the city and nearby, often on lines raised above the streets. Driverless trains also haul cars in quarries, mines, and factories.

Signs of Trouble

Driverless trains have onboard computers programmed with their routes and station stops. They also have satnav and similar technology, and radio links to a central control room. On-train sensors record speed and direction, whether there are problems with the motors, wheels, or other parts, and even how much shaking or vibration there is, which could reveal a cracked rail or chipped wheel.

Central Control

All the information from the train sensors is updated and sent to central control. Here people keep an eye on the entire train network. Each time a train stops at a station, its equipment is checked automatically. In addition, sensors along the tracks detect each train's passing, the time, and how fast it is going.

Safe Systems

Wherever people and robots get together, safety is vital. On a robot railway, if one part breaks down or fails, there are at least two backups ready to take over. If a train runs over an accidentally broken rail, the track signals automatically stop other trains coming near. The system is designed to be fail-safe. Even if the electric supply fails, the people and trains stay safe.

 *In a robot railway control room, people keep a constant check on the trains, signals, points, and video cameras, to make sure everything is working properly.*

Robot trains often travel above city streets, away from cars and people. The Las Vegas Monorail has a track more than 3.7 miles (6 km) long.

ROBOT SUPERSTAR

Train Pusher

*Few robots match Elbrams for size and power. Each Elbram is an automatic train pusher that weighs more than 55 tons (50 t). It runs on rails, has diesel engines, and two arms worked by **hydraulics**. One arm grabs the rail and pushes along, then lets go as the other one takes over, and so on—like pulling hand-over-hand on a rope. Elbram can roll a train weighing 11,000 tons (10,000 t).*

The Sky's the Limit

"Hello, this is your **autopilot** George speaking. Today I will be flying you across the ocean, while the human pilots have a snack and a nap. Don't worry. We work as a team and do it every day."

Help in the Cockpit

Robot autopilots do not have total control in planes that carry people. They help the human pilots. Big passenger planes have an autopilot, which is part of the computer-based flight management system (FMS). This determines where the plane is, where it is going, and the best route to avoid storms and other dangers. Once the human pilots have set the autopilot, they can relax. But they still keep an eye on the controls and displays, just in case anything goes wrong. Lights flash and beepers sound if there is a problem.

Knowing the Way

An autopilot uses a satnav system as one source of information. Radio beacons on the ground that send out coded radio signals about their location are another source. Most planes also have an inertial navigation system (INS) which contains machines that measure the plane's speed and direction very accurately (see page 21).

▼ *Once the autopilot is set on a modern passenger plane, the flight crew can spend time planning ahead or double-checking that all is well.*

 The Heron robot spy plane carries several kinds of cameras and other sensors. It is about the size of a two-seater aircraft and can stay in the sky for more than two days.

Taking Measurements

How does INS work? If you are in a car that suddenly goes faster, or accelerates, you are pressed back in your seat. As you turn a corner, you tend to lean sideways. INS **accelerometers** measure a plane's speed and changes of direction very accurately, second by second. There is also usually a **gyroscope**—a fast-spinning wheel or ball that stays in a steady position, always pointing the same way as the aircraft turns, climbs, or descends. The computer combines information from these INS devices to determine how far the plane has traveled and in which direction.

Planes without Pilots

Some aircraft have no pilots at all. They are fully robotic or **autonomous**, guided by an onboard computer using satnav information. These types of robo-planes include military spy **drones** that take photographs of army headquarters, air bases, and naval ports.

In the comedy film *Airplane* (1980), the autopilot is called Otto, rather than George, and he's an inflatable dummy, rather than a real pilot.

ROBOT SUPERSTAR

George

The autopilot of an airplane is traditionally known as George. This might be after George DeBeeson who improved autopilot design in the 1920s. Or it could refer to the gyroscope part of the autopilot. In the alphabet pilots use, the word Golf stands for the letter G, but the word for G used to be George. The pilot said, "Let George do it," meaning that the gyroscope autopilot was taking over.

Robo-boats

Robot watercraft on rivers, lakes, and seas face many dangers. They could hit rocks, get stuck in shallows, bump into another boat, capsize, or even sink beneath the waves.

ROBOT OR NOT?

Self-steering

Some boats have self-steering or autohelm, like a simple autopilot. The crew sets the angle between a flag-like wind vane and the steering rudder. If the boat changes course, a lever system moves the rudder so the boat turns back to the correct angle. There are also versions with a magnetic compass and GPS. But these are not real robots. They cannot decide to change course, start or stop, detect when the wind direction alters, or avoid obstacles. However, they do give the boat crew a rest.

Cruising the Ocean

Beagle B is 3.8 yards (3.5 m) long and can travel for weeks on a course programmed into its computer. This robot sailing dinghy detects the strength and direction of the wind and the depth of the water it is floating in, using echo-sounding or sonar. It can also tell whether it is upright or leaning. Beagle B has a magnetic compass and a GPS satnav receiver, as well as solar panels, which charge its batteries. These power the computer and the electric motors that move the rudder and sail.

The robot sailing dinghy Beagle B cruises around, taking water samples to test in its onboard mini-laboratory.

Across the Atlantic?

Pinta, Roboboat Mark III, *and other small robotic boats are designed to sail all the way across the Atlantic Ocean in about three months. Most of them have sails, an onboard computer, and solar panels for electricity. They are testing the idea that one day, large sailing ships could carry cargo across the ocean without a crew or fuel.*

Cleaner Means Faster

Seaweed and small sea creatures, such as limpets and barnacles, grow on the hulls of ships and boats. Cleaning them off allows boats to go faster and use less fuel. The small robot cleaner HISMAR (hull identification system for marine autonomous robotics) crawls over the hull of boats, blasting off growths with powerful water jets. The cleaner determines the quickest route to clean the hull, while avoiding parts such as the propeller or water intakes.

Cleaning ship and boat hulls usually means they must come out of the water into a dry dock. Robot hull cleaners work while the boat is still in the water.

Move Like an Animal

The most successful movers in the animal world are insects. There are millions of different kinds, all with six legs. Spiders, with eight legs, also go almost everywhere. Snakes and worms may be legless, but they are great movers, too. Robots can copy all these creatures.

Stand Up, Fall Over

Six legs or more on a robot are useful, because even if three lift off the ground, the others keep the robot well balanced and stable. The robot moves a few legs at a time and steps along without falling over. If a robot had four straight legs—one at each corner—it would topple, if it lifted even one of the legs. Successful four-legged (or quadruped) robots can bend their other three legs to tilt the body over them and stay standing. This type of robot needs delicate balance sensors, which can detect the downward pull of **gravity** and how much the robot tilts or leans. The sensors are connected to fast-acting electric motors that work the legs.

▶▶ *The Genghis series of mini-robots is designed to test different ways of walking. One of the most successful designs has six legs, like the real insect shown here, which is a cricket.*

Robots in Action∎

METAL MUSCLES

Robo-lobster is about the size of a big
real-life lobster. It is designed to crawl
along the sea bed on eight legs, to detect
explosive mines and other dangers. It does
not have electric motors like ordinary
robots, since these do not work if they get
wet. Instead it has "metal muscles" or shape-
shifting wires that shorten when electricity
passes through them. When the electricity
stops, the wires lengthen again. The metal
muscles move Robo-lobster's legs in the
same way as a real lobster.∎

Ninja is a 4-legged robot
with 20 suckers on each foot.
These allow it to climb smooth
surfaces and even crawl up
windows, to check the glass and
other items, such as wires and pipes.

Running Robots

Walk over there, run back here, jog for a while, hop and skip, leap and jump. We humans can move in many ways on two legs or even one—it's so natural and easy. But for robots, bipedal or two-legged travel is an enormous problem.

In the Balance

We humans have a very good sense of balance, and our muscles react quickly, so we don't fall over even when we stand on one leg. We are, in effect, one-legged for about two-thirds of the time when walking, because we lift up each foot in turn and move it forward. It's tricky to build a robot with gravity detectors, accelerometers, and other sensors that are delicate enough and work fast enough to power electric motors and move mechanical legs as quickly as human ones.

Small and Simple

Runbot is a small robot less than 12 inches (30 cm) tall. It is two legs and not much else. Each hip has a small electric motor, and so does each knee. There are sensors to measure the angles of these joints, how upright Runbot is, and how hard each foot presses down. The angle or slope of the ground is measured by an infrared beam.

Leaning to Walk

A clever feature of Runbot is its "brain." This is not one single computer but several sets of electronic **circuits** and **microchips**. If Runbot takes small steps and starts to lean forward too far, the circuits work together to detect this and lengthen its stride. In this way, Runbot can learn to walk and run, go uphill and down, and handle uneven ground.

A toddler shows that humans find learning to walk quite difficult and have plenty of trips and falls. Bipedal robots have similar problems.

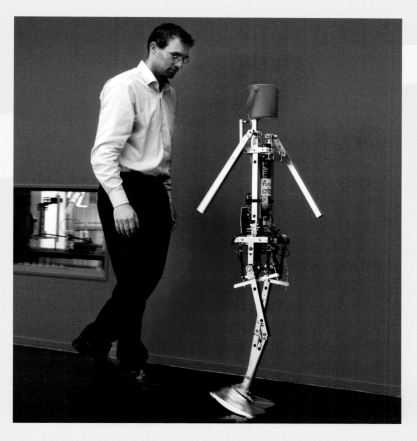

◀◀ *The two-legged robot Denise (the knees) tests out new kinds of leg joints and balance sensors. Walking robots have improved greatly since the late 1990s.*

ROBOT OR NOT?
○○○

Extra Power

*The human body has a framework of bones inside called an **endoskeleton** (meaning skeleton inside). Robot engineers make bigger frameworks of metal and plastic called **exoskeletons** (meaning skeleton outside), like a mechanical suit to fit around the person's head, body, arms, and legs. As the human inside moves, the exoskeleton copies the actions but with much greater strength, using powerful electric motors or even a car engine! Are these powered exoskeletons true robots? Not really—they are under human control and don't work by themselves or make decisions.*

This exoskeleton is worn by divers underwater. It gives them extra strength to help them move heavy objects.

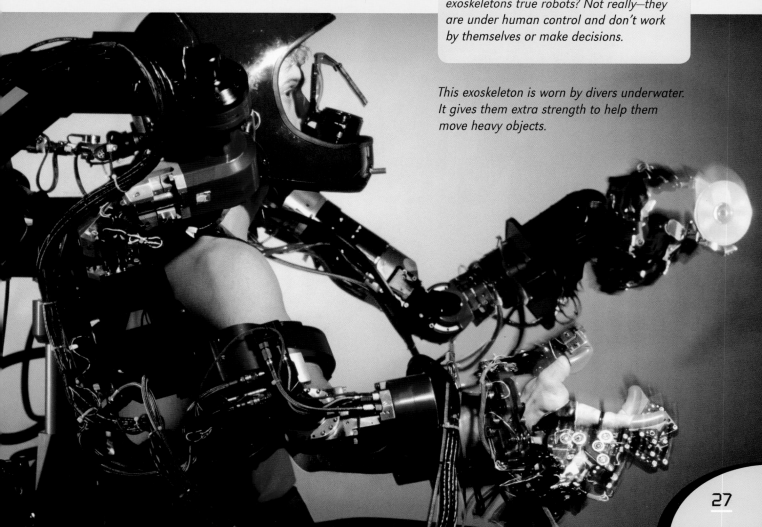

Going Places

Mobile robots move in very strange ways even when they fall over! Tetwalkers look like pyramids made of tubes with three sides and a base. They change shape by making their tubes shorter or longer, which lets them move by toppling or somersaulting along.

Four-sided Robot

A single tetwalker has four sides, each one a triangle. This shape is called a **tetrahedron**, hence the name tetwalker. The sides are made of hollow tubes that slide into each other so they can shorten or lengthen, like telescopes. Electric motors at the corners where the sides join, or in the middle of each side, make this happen.

Robots in Action■

NANOBOTS

The smallest robots, nanobots, are too tiny to see except through a microscope. Being so little, they are quite simple. Joining together many slightly different nanobots can make a larger, quite complicated robot—perhaps as big as this letter "o"!■

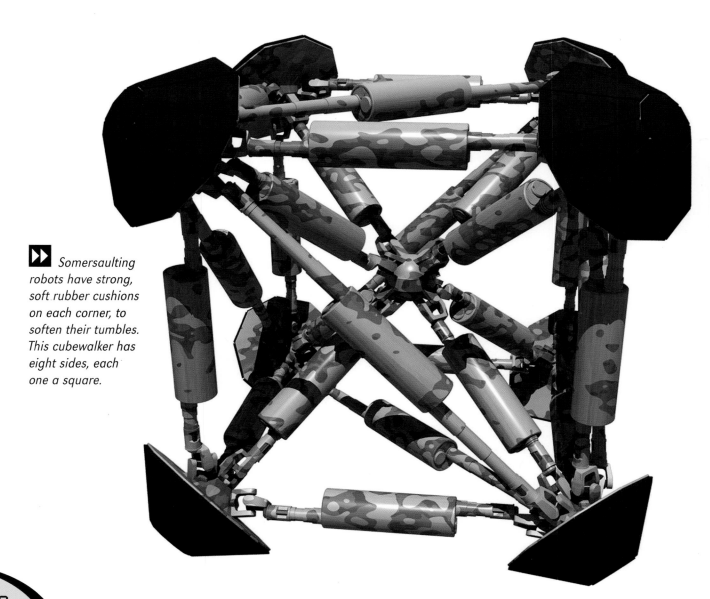

▶▶ *Somersaulting robots have strong, soft rubber cushions on each corner, to soften their tumbles. This cubewalker has eight sides, each one a square.*

Shape-shifter

When a tetwalker moves, three sides become longer while the other shortens. The tetwalker grows taller, leans to one side and flops over. The sides change their lengths again, and the same thing happens. It's not so much tetwalking as tet-tumbling. A computer controls the electric motors. By changing which sides grow longer or shorter, the tetwalker can alter direction, zigzag, or go in reverse. And it can cope with lumps and bumps, soft ground such as sand or loose pebbles, as well as slopes.

Tiny Tets

In the future, lots of very tiny tetwalkers called **nanotets** could be linked into groups or swarms, all tumbling along together. Their small onboard computers could also be linked. If the leading members of the group came upon a blockage or obstacle, the computers would decide between them which way they should all steer to go around it. These huge groups could become self-controlling or autonomous, known as autonomous nanotechnology swarms (ANTS).

Tetwalkers are being tested as robots to send into space. They could move across rough ground on other planets, unlike the usual wheeled rovers.

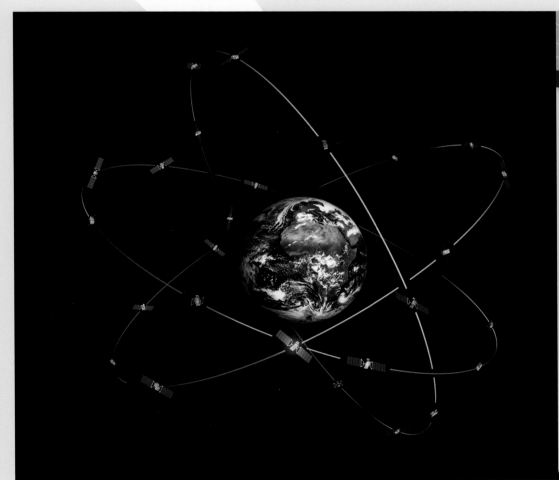

ROBO-FUTURE

Better GPS

European space scientists are building a new satnav system called Galileo. This should allow ships, boats, planes, cars, and trains find their position to the nearest yard (meter), rather than several yards (meters) as with GPS. In a few years, robots could use both GPS and Galileo to know where they are and navigate much more precisely.

Glossary

accelerometer
A device that measures movement, especially how quickly something speeds up (accelerates) or slows down (decelerates).

autonomous
When a machine or device mainly controls itself and works on its own, without human control, as most robots do.

autopilot
Automatic pilot: a machine that steers and controls an aircraft for a set amount of time, but that can be switched off if there is a problem, so human pilots can take over.

circuit
In electrical equipment, a circuit is the path or route of electricity through various wires, switches, microchips, and other parts.

cog
A wheel with pointed teeth around the edge, sometimes called a gearwheel or cogwheel, found on bicycles and in many robots. (see gears).

drones
Robot planes with no human crew, which people program or instruct to fly to a specific place, perhaps to take photographs or to spy on others.

endoskeleton
A strong supporting framework on the inside of an animal or machine, such as the skeleton of bones inside the human body.

exoskeleton
A strong supporting framework on the outside of an animal or machine, such as the hard outer body casing of a beetle.

gears
Two or more wheels with pointed teeth around the edges, called cogs, cogwheels, or gearwheels. They have teeth that interlock or mesh together so that one wheel turns the next (see cog).

GPS
Stands for Global Positioning System: this is made up of more than 20 satellites, which travel around Earth and send out radio signals detected by a GPS receiver. They show the position, or location, of the receiver and help find the way or navigate. GPS is often called satnav (see navigation).

gravity
The natural pulling force that affects all objects, from pieces of dust to stars, and attracts other objects. The bigger or more massive an object, the stronger its gravity.

gyroscope
A very fast-spinning wheel or ball that resists being moved or tilted and tries to say in the same position.

hydraulic
When a liquid under pressure, such as oil or water, is pumped into a pipe to create a pushing force at the other end.

infrared light
Light with waves slightly longer than red light waves, which our eyes cannot see, but which some animals' eyes can. Used in devices such as remote controls for TVs and robots.

laser beams
Beams of very powerful light that do not spread out or widen, unlike ordinary light beams.

locomotory robots
Robots that locomote or move around, traveling from one place to another, rather than staying in the same place.

microchip
A small wafer or flat piece of a substance such as silicon, with thousands of microscopic electronic parts on its surface.

nanotets
Very tiny tetrahedrons (see tetrahedron), even smaller than the dot on this letter "i."

navigation
Finding the way or route while traveling on a journey from one place to another.

pivot
Swing around or tilt or spin.

pneumatic tires
Hollow tires filled with air under high pressure, like those on bicycles and cars.

pulses
Short bursts or amounts with gaps between, such as a light that flashes on and off many times.

reduction gears
Gearwheels that reduce spinning or turning speed, when a small gearwheel with few teeth links or meshes with a large gearwheel with many teeth, so the large one turns more slowly than the small one (see gears).

satnav
Stands for satellite navigation: finding the way using a GPS receiver that detects radio signals from satellites going around Earth (see GPS and navigation).

sensors
Devices that detect something, such as light, sound, touch, heat, or certain chemicals.

tetrahedron
A shape with four flat sides, each of which is a triangle.

torque
A measurement of the turning or twisting power or strength of a machine.

ultrasound
Sounds that are too high pitched and shrill for human ears to hear, but which some animals and devices can detect.

Further Reading

Ferrari, Mario. *Building Robots with LEGO Mindstorms NXT.* Rockland: Syngress, 2007.

Gifford, Clive. *Robots.* New York: Atheneum, 2008.

Hyland, Tony. *How Robots Work. Robots and Robotics.* North Mankato: Smart Apple Media, 2008.

Piddock, Charles. *Future Tech: From Personal Robots to Motorized Monocycles.* Washington, D.C.: National Geographic, 2009.

Strom, Laura Layton. *From Bugbots to Humanoids: Robotics.* Shockwave. New York: Children's Press, 2008.

Web Sites

RoboGames
RoboGames is the site for U.S. games where the best minds from around the world compete in over 70 different events. Combat robots, walking humanoids, soccer bots, sumo bots, and even androids that do kung fu. Some robots are autonomous, some are remote controlled.
www.robogames.net

Robot Video Clips
Robot Video Clips shows video clips of all kinds of robots in action.
www.robotclips.com

Robot World News
Robot World News covers the top news stories on robotics, artificial intelligence, and related areas, plus fun information on robots such as toys.
www.robotworldnews.com

Index